MUSLIM BOYS

MANNERS IN MADEENAH

ABU-BAKR NURI

MUSLIM BOYS

MANNERS IN MADEENAH

ABU-BAKR NURI

Dedication

'(Our Lord! Accept this from us; You are the All-Hearing, the All-Knowing).'

(The Qur'aan: Chapter 2, Verse 127)

Abu-Bakr

Hobby: Computer Coding
Role: Leader
Nature: Gentle
Carries: Backpack

Umar

Hobby: Karate
Role: Guard
Nature: Tough
Carries: Belt

Uthmaan

Hobby: Parkour
Role: Mapper
Nature: Cool
Carries: Ball

Ali

Hobby: Fencing
Role: Planner
Nature: Mild
Carries: Sword

It all started on a Sunday morning; four boys went running towards their neighborhood park. They didn't notice the black suburban utility vehicle (SUV) parked on the corner of the street. The boys were having a race; but as he was running down Abu-Bakr was grabbed by someone and taken into the car. Umar was left wondering where he went but as he was running *SNATCH,* he was pulled in too. Uthmaan saw Umar being snatched into the car, so he tried to halt himself to a stop; however

Ali wasn't paying as much attention and he pushed Uthmaan towards the car by accident. Moments later all four of them were in the car.

The boys tried to ask questions only to be told to be silent. Whilst

they sat quietly, confused and not knowing what to expect, they noticed an old man appear and he too entered the SUV. The boys had no clue what was in store for them. They sat patiently as the old man began to speak.

"Assalaamu 'alaykum, you four have been chosen for a special mission. Your mission is to get three hadeeths; if you get them, apply them to your lives, and teach others about them you will be successful, *in shaa'Allaah*. You can't waste time though. Someone else is seeking to destroy them. His name is Talhah. Then the hadeeths will be

lost forever!" concluded the old man. "By the way, my name is, Adab."

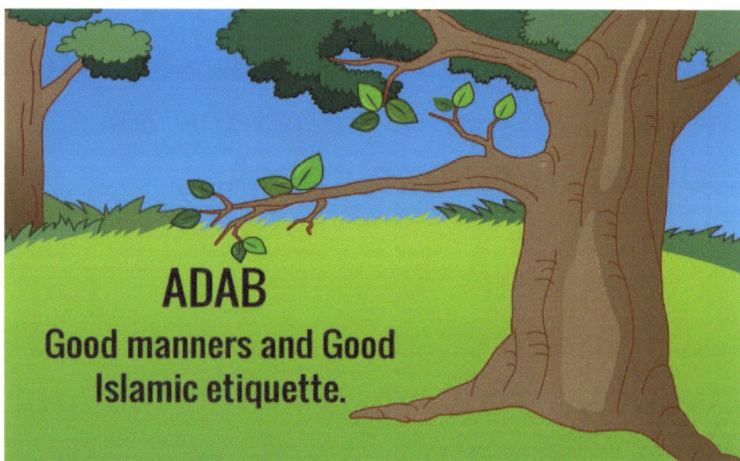

ADAB
Good manners and Good Islamic etiquette.

"Adab, what a beautiful name maa shaa' Allaah," said Uthmaan. "It means good manners and good Islamic etiquette," he added. They all smiled.

"Now all you have to do is take this package with you and review it. Everything you need for this journey is in this package; tickets, information on your car and driver," said Adab. And without another word he left.

"Really?" Umar said. They all looked at each other and decided to open the package and see what was inside. Just as Adab had said, the tickets were there, the information about the car and the driver, and their destination; they were going to Madeenah! Uthmaan was so excited, "What will we tell our parents?"

Abu-Bakr right then read, "Tell your parents that you are going to Madeenah - all expenses paid!" He was so excited he forgot that they actually had a job to do on this trip. They ran home and begged their parents for permission. The parents agreed Alhamdullilah.

They were booked on the next flight. This was going to be a short trip and they were each given a backpack with some clothes and necessities. They prayed Dhuhr and Asr at the airport.

Thirty hours later they reached a little city outside of Madeenah and were on the camels headed towards what looked like the guy who had the first hadeeth, Jamal. Five minutes barely passed when they came to a market place. They quickly got down and

began inspecting each of the stalls.Umar found a water stall, and with Abu-Bakr's help, bought eight water bottles.

Ali on the other hand was keeping an eye out for Talhah; he was the one who wanted to destroy the hadeeths. Sure enough, Ali managed to spot him and described him to the others. They all agreed this was the Talhah they had been warned about. They quickly ducked behind different barrels and began looking at the writing on them so people wouldn't become suspicious. Meanwhile, Talhah

was eating food from the stalls without paying for it. The owners of the stalls became angry and started chasing him.

He was caught red-handed; and on the consent of the stall keepers, they took him to the police station where he was thrown in jail.

Ali, who was a skilled sword fighter, purchased a sword and took that with him for protection. While everyone had their eyes focused on Talhah, someone moved unnoticed.

Abu-Bakr had crept to the camels and prepared them for riding. He signaled to the other boys to come. They quickly ran to him. They mounted on the camels and rode off.

Uthmaan soon began to feel thirsty and asked Ali for some water. They all stopped and drank the water, which was still cool. The camels slowly went on. It was getting dark and they needed to pray, so they made wudoo' using the water bottles and began to pray Maghrib and Isha.

After praying, they rested under a grove of palm trees given to the public. Abu-Bakr took off his slippers and began climbing up one of the trees; he had found a few coconuts. He threw them down to the other boys and slid down and began climbing up another tree. This time it was a date tree, and he passed the

dates to the boys. Then he came down and they broke the coconuts and ate the dates.

After they tied their camels to the tree, they dozed off.

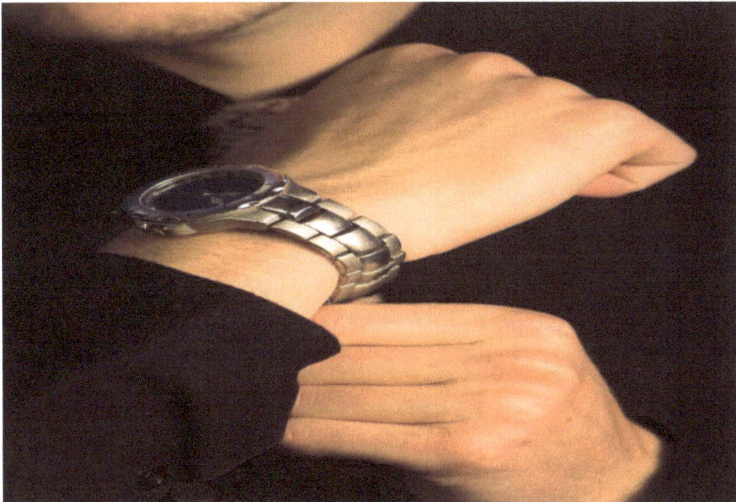

Beep, beep, beep...,' Ali's alarm on his watch was going off and they all got woken up abruptly. It

was time for the Fajr salaah; they used some water from the water bottle to make wudoo' and prayed together. Abu-Bakr led the salaah, because he had memorized the most Qur'aan, and when they were done they began to move on.

Alhamdulillaah, they had finally reached Madeenah.

Meanwhile, Talhah began pacing around his prison room; he had an idea! He quickly picked up his spoon from lunch and began prying out one of the bricks. It was really hard but he was determined to break free, he

finally succeeded in getting one out and it fell down.

Back in Madeenah Uthmaan greeted the first man he saw and asked where Jamal's house was. The man gave him directions and they set off towards the house.

Talhah succeeded in getting out two more large bricks, before making his escape. As soon as he was out he looked for a horse. Seconds later he stole one and was on his way to Madeenah.

Meanwhile, the boys arrived at Jamal's house. Ali knocked three times and waited. A young man, between the age of 30 and 40 years old, opened the door. Umar asked in a questioning voice, "Jamal?"

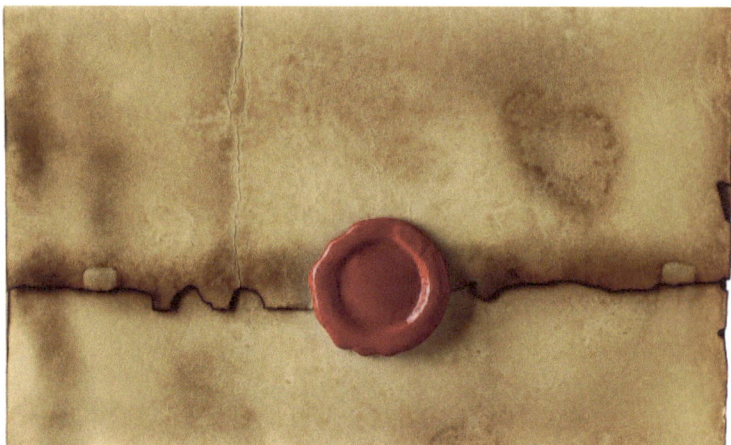

Jamal laughed and answered, "Yes?" Abu-Bakr then asked him for a hadeeth on manners. Jamal retreated back into the house and brought back a script, inscribed on it was the hadeeth.

They exchanged greetings and left his house quickly.

As Talhah neared Madeenah, he wondered whether the boys had obtained the script or not. As he was thinking that, the boys were riding out of Madeenah. Uthmaan spotted him, but before he could say anything, Talhah was riding towards them as fast as he could. Abu-Bakr frantically tried to outrun him, but the horse was faster than the camel. They all got down and prepared to fight.

Talhah got off his horse and began a duel. Ali was the only one with a sword and fought with him for five minutes, but Talhah was also skilled and it began to become clear that this would be a draw. Finally, Talhah called a draw and as soon as he said that, Umar sprang to his feet and put him in a headlock. Meanwhile Abu-Bakr hit Talhah's horse on the rear so it would run away.

Uthmaan quickly put the camels together and called all of the boys to climb aboard. Umar released Talhah and speeded towards the camel. Talhah fell down and just gazed at the sky.

He did not know in which direction they left, for he was dizzy on the floor for a few minutes.

As they speeded to where they first mounted the camel, they found the same marketplace they had passed by earlier. The stall keepers asked, "Where is Talhah?" Abu-Bakr informed them and three stall keepers raced to go and get him.

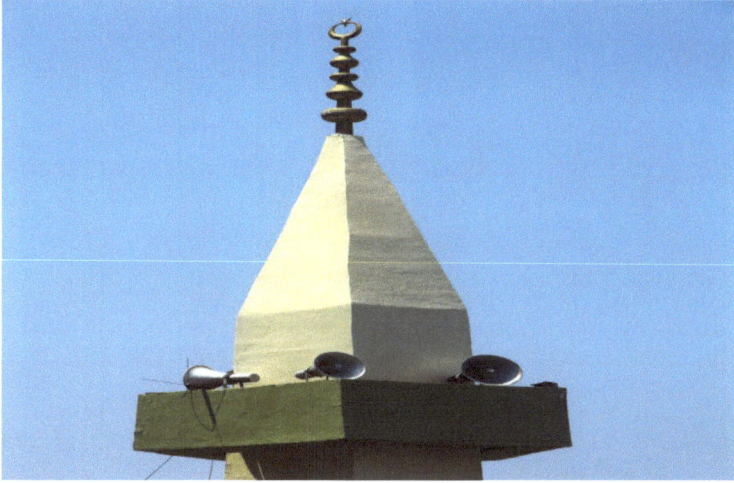

Right then they heard the adhaan for Dhuhr salaah, and they all made wudoo' quickly and prayed Dhuhr and Asr salaah together.

Ali checked and informed the others that they had one more minute to go and they would be home free.

They reached the same place where they had arrived and got in the car together, headed for the airport.

They were back in the black SUV. Adab thanked them profusely and let them go back home.

They opened the script, read it out aloud and felt amazed.

The hadeeth was as follows: The Prophet Muhammad (peace and blessings of Allaah be upon him) said:

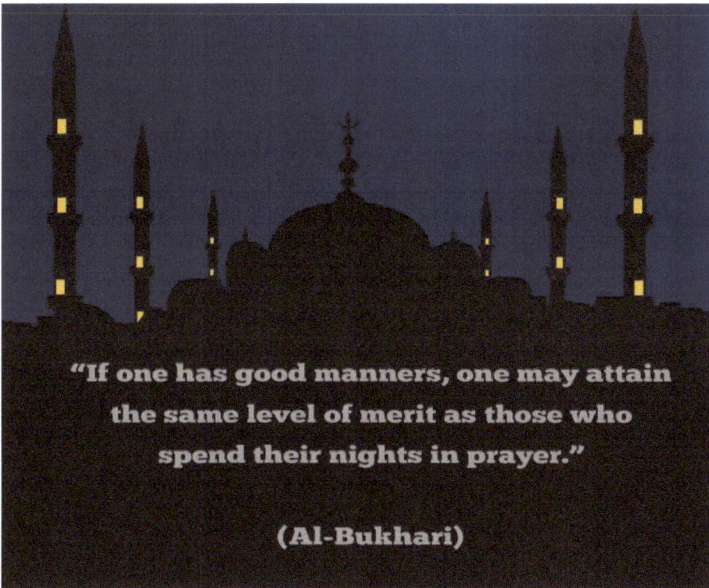

"If one has good manners, one may attain the same level of merit as those who spend their nights in prayer."

(Al-Bukhari)

Then, they went back to their houses. They had a lot to think about. Meanwhile, Talhah was once again caught and thrown into jail.

All four boys realized that having good manners is very important and they needed to apply this hadeeth in their lives. They knew this would be difficult to do, but in shaa'Allaah if they tried Allaah would make it easy for them.

Have You Bought The Series: "Things Every Kid Should Know: Amr's Adventure in Europe, Drugs, Alcohol, Smoking, Bullying and Junk Food" for Your Kids By Alya Nuri?

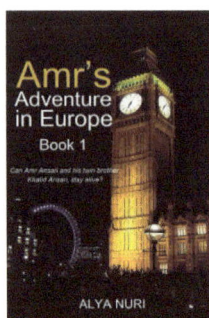

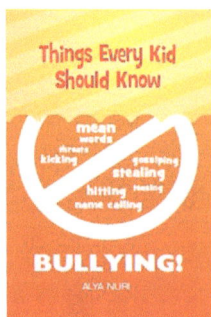

Have You Bought The Series: "Things Every Kid Should Know: Strangers and Fire" for Your Kids By Zafar (Abu-Bakr) Nuri?

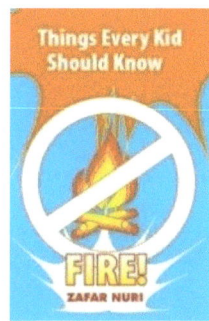

Have You Bought The Series: "Things Every Kid Should Know: Hand Washing" for Your Kids By Arsalon (Umar) Nuri?

www.ingramcontent.com/pod-product-compliance
Lightning Source LLC
Chambersburg PA
CBHW041306020426
42331CB00001B/1